KALIDASA

RITUSAMHARA
THE SIX SEASONS

Also by Abhay K.

Poetry Collections

Enigmatic Love
Fallen Leaves of Autumn
Candling the Light
Remains
The Seduction of Delhi
The Eight-eyed Lord of Kathmandu
The Prophecy of Brasilia
The Alphabets of Latin America
The Magic of Madagascar

Edited Books

CAPITALS
100 Great Indian Poems
100 More Great Indian Poems
New Brazilian Poems
The Bloomsbury Anthology of Great Indian Poems
100 Grandes Poemas da Índia
Cien Grandes Poemas de la India
100 Grandi Poesie Indiane
Tononkalo Indianina 100 Tsara Indriandra
100 Grands Poèmes Indiens
The Bloomsbury Book of Great Indian Love Poems

Translated Books

Meghaduta by Kalidasa

Memoirs

River Valley to Silicon Valley
The Colours of Soul

KALIDASA

RITUSAMHARA

THE SIX SEASONS

Translated by

ABHAY K.

B L O O M S B U R Y

NEW DELHI • LONDON • OXFORD • NEW YORK • SYDNEY

BLOOMSBURY INDIA
Bloomsbury Publishing India Pvt Ltd
Second Floor, LSC Building No. 4, DDA Complex, Pocket C – 6 & 7,
Vasant Kunj, New Delhi 110070

BLOOMSBURY, BLOOMSBURY INDIA and the Diana logo
are trademarks of Bloomsbury Publishing Plc

First published in India 2021
This edition published 2021

ISBN: PB: 978-93-54350-02-3; e-book: 978-93-54350-18-4

2 4 6 8 10 9 7 5 3 1

Printed and bound in India by Replika Press Pvt Ltd

PRAISE FOR ABHAY K.'s TRANSLATION OF *RITUSAMHARA*

"Abhay K. has awakened the love-god from deep slumber."

Gabriel Rosenstock, Ireland

"I have read and published several translations of *Ritusamhara* over the years but this is unquestionably the most wonderful. Most versions in existence are rigid and scholarly. In the process, they have lost out on the magic and enchantment of the original. Abhay K., being a poet, captures precisely that. This is the Kalidasa you want to read."

– Pritish Nandy

INTRODUCTION

Ecopoetry is the new buzzword. As the world faces biodiversity loss of unprecedented scale with around one million species on the verge of extinction, poetry with a strong ecological content has started to take the centre stage of contemporary poetic discourse. New anthologies of ecopoems are getting published every year. Some notable ones are *Wild Reckoning* edited by John Burnside and Maurice Riordon (2004), *The Thunder Mutters: 101 Poems for the Planet* edited by Alice Oswald (2005), *Earth Shattering: Ecopoems* edited by Neil Asteley (2007) and *Redstart: An Ecological Poetics* edited by Forrest Gander and John Kinsella (2012).

The description of *Earth Shattering* states—"This is the first anthology to show the full range of ecopoetry, from the wilderness poetry of ancient China to 21st-century native American poetry, with postcolonial and feminist perspectives represented by writers such as Derek Walcott, Ernesto Cardinal, Oodgeroo and Susan Griffin." However, Indian ecopoetry finds no mention here although *Meghaduta* and *Ritusamhara* by Kalidasa are some of the finest examples of ecopoetry.

Kalidasa's *Ritusamhara* describes changing life in six seasons—Summer, Rains, Autumn, Frost, Winter and Spring, by making reference to a wide variety of flora and fauna and their interaction with the environment.

Kalidasa emerges as an ecopoet of very high sensibility and consciousness as he describes the plight of animals in different seasons in *Ritusamhara* and how they come together to support each other during extreme weather conditions while keeping their natural instincts at bay. For example in Summer—

हुताग्निकल्पैः सवितुर्गभस्तिभिः
कलापिनः क्लान्तशरीरचेतसाः।
न भोगिनम् घ्नन्ति समीपवर्तिनम्
कलापचक्रेषु निवेशिताननम्।। १-१६

Peacocks, their bodies and souls wilting under the sun's
piercing rays like the flames of sacred ritual fire,
wedge their heads into the discs of their dazzling plumes
and do not kill the serpents slithering nearby. 1-16

विवस्वता तीक्ष्णतरांशुमालिना
सपङ्कतोयात् सरसोऽभितापिताः।
उत्प्लुत्य भेकस्तृषितस्य भोगिनाः
फणातपत्रस्य तले निषीदति।। १-१८

Singed by the scorching sun rays
frogs leap out of the muddy marshand
sit under the hood parasol
of a tired and thirsty cobra. 1-18

German philosopher Martin Heidegger thought that the function of poetry is to save the Earth from the consequences of an instrumental or technological attitude towards nature. Kalidasa's poetry exactly does that.

I have not come across any other poet who describes the lives of antelopes, peacocks, boars, lions, elephants, cobras, frogs and buffaloes in such detail and with such empathy. In *Ritusamhara*, Kalidasa continues to delight us with these vivid descriptions of plants, insects and flowers in the rainy season—

प्रभिन्नवैदूर्यनिभैस् तृणाङ्कुरैः
समाचिताप्रोत्थितकन्दलीदलैः।
विभाति शुक्लेतररत्नभूषिता
वाराङ्गनेव क्षितिर् इन्द्रगोपकैः।। २-५

Like jade fragments, the green grass rises
spreading its blades to catch raindrops,
red Indragopaka insects perch on fresh
leaf-buds bursting forth from the Kandali plants
the earth smiles like an elegant lady
draped in nature's colourful jewels. 2-5

How rains and clouds are equally important in making even nature alive with joy, what of humans then?

वनद्विपानाम् नववारिदस्वनैर्
मदान्वितानाम् ध्वनताम् मुहुर् मुहुः।
कपोलदेशा विमलोत्पलप्रभाः
सभृङ्गयूथैर् मदवारिभिश् चिता।। २-१५

Wild rutting elephants trumpet incessantly
as if challenging the thundering clouds,
their secreting temples resemble dark blue lotuses
and are frequented by hosts of honey bees. 2-15

The magnificence of Indragopaka insects and Kandali plants would be lost without these stanzas of Kalidasa. *Ritusamhara* shows the splendour and majesty of all these species in their finest glory and exhorts us to do all we can to protect and preserve them.

In *Ritusamhara*, Autumn begins with Kasa blossoms, silver moon, white Hamsas, blooming lilies and fragrant white jasmine. Now, let's consider a modern megapolis of today, concrete buildings all around, streets choking with cars and polluted air to bretahe. How does one perceive the change in seasons? Kalidasa's verses in *Ritusamhara* tell us that we are heading in the wrong direction. We must slow down and look back at Kasa blossoms, the silver moon, white Hamsas, blooming lilies, fragrant white jasmine and preserve them for our generation and for the generations to come.

काशैर्मही शिशिरदीधितिना रजन्यो
हंसैर् जलानि सरिताम् कुमुदैः सरांसि।
सप्तच्चदैः कुसुमभारनतैर् वनान्ताः
शुक्लीकृतान्य् उपवनानि च मालतीभिः।। ३–२

The earth wrapped in white Kasa blossoms,
nights lit up with the silver moon,
river currents white with Hamsas
and ponds filled with white lilies,
forests—teeming with Saptachadda plants
bowing gently with the weight of their flowers,
gardens fragrant with white Malati blossoms,
white reigns all around, pleasing our eyes. 3-2

दिवसकरमयूखैर् बोध्यमानम् प्रभाते
वरयुवतिमुखाभम् पङ्कजम् जृम्भतेऽद्य।
कुमुदम् अपि गतेऽस्तम् लीयते चन्द्रबिम्बे
हसितम् इव वधूनाम् प्रोषितेषु प्रियेषु।। ३–२३

Aroused by the sun rays at sunrise,
Pankaja opens up like glowing face
of a young woman, while the moon
turns pale, smile vanishes from Kumuda
like that of the young women,
after their lovers are gone far away. 3-23

In the season of frost, Kalidasa underlines the importance of powders, incense, perfumes obtained from various plants in enhancing women's beauty and the role of plants and animals in arousing passion in the young hearts.

गात्राणि कालीयकचर्चितानि
सपत्रलेखानि मुखाम्बुजानि।
शिरांसि कालागुरुधूपितानि
कुर्वन्ति नार्यः सुरतोत्सवाय।। ४-५

Young women rub Kalakeya perfumed powder
on their bodies and tattoo their lotus like faces
with flower patterns, and perfume their hair
with the incense of Kakaguru as they get ready
for the joyous carnival of lovemaking. 4-5

Kalakeya: Fragrant turmeric powder
Kakaguru: Resins of Aloe Vera

प्रभूतशालिप्रसवैश्चितानि
मृगाङ्गनायूथविभूषितानि।
मनोहरक्रौञ्चनिनादितानि
सीमान्तराण्य् उत्सुकयन्ति चेतः।। ४-८

The fields covered with ripened paddy
as far as eyes can see, their boundaries
full of herd of does, midlands filled with
sweet cries of graceful demoiselle cranes.
Ah! What passion they arouse in the heart! 4-8

In Winter too, women drink flower wine, eat betel rolls, wear colourful silks and fragrant flowers. It seems impossible to express love without the flora and fauna surrounding them. For example, who would fill our hearts with passion in the absence of demoiselles cranes, herd of does, fragrance of jasmine flowers and Kalaguru incense?

गृहीतताम्बूलविलेपनस्रजः
मुखासवामोदितवक्त्रपङ्कजाः।
प्रकामकालागुरुधूपवासितं
विशन्ति शय्यागृहम् उत्सुकाः स्त्रियः।। ५-५

Women aching for love, their mouths perfumed
with flower-wine, retire to their bedchambers
filled with fragrance of Kalaguru incense, carrying
betel rolls, chaplets and sensuous perfumes. 5-5

Kalaguru: Black Aloeswood

मनोज्ञकूर्पासकपीडितस्तनाः
सरागकौशेयकभूषितोरसः।
निवेशितान्तः कुसुमैः शिरोरुहैर्
विभूषयन्तीव हिमागमम् स्त्रियः।। ५-८

Dazzling like jewels—their voluptuous breasts
held tightly by lovely bodices, their sensuous thighs
covered in colourful silks, fragrant flowers adorning
their hair—women welcome the winter's arrival. 5-8

Spring arrives like a warrior armed with spiky mango blossoms and humming bees. Who but the ecopoet in Kalidasa can imagine spring as a warrior whose weapons are fresh blossoms and humming of bees, when women's sensuality is enhanced by fresh blooms of Karnikara, Ashoka and Navamallika flowers—

कर्णेषु योग्यम् नवकर्णिकारं
चलेषु नीलेष्व् अलकेष्व् अशोकम्।
पुष्पम् च फुल्लम् नवमल्लिकाया:
प्रयाति कान्तिम् मदाजनानाम्।। ६-५

Fresh blooms of Karnikara on their ears,
a chaplet of Ashoka flowers and full blooms
of Navamallika vines on their curly dark hair,
magnify the sensuality of beautiful women. 6-5

पुंस्कोकिलश्चूतरसासवेन
मत्तः प्रियाम् चुम्बति रागहृष्टः।
कूजद्द्विरेफोऽप्य् अयम् अम्बुजस्थः
प्रियम् प्रियायाः प्रकरोति चाटु।। ६-१४

Crazy cuckoo drunk on Mango nectar,
kisses his mate passionately,
so do the honey bees hidden inside lotus petals,
make love to their sweethearts. 6-14

In *Redstart*, Forrest Gander and John Kinsella ask—"The damage humans have perpetrated on our environment has certainly affected a poet's means and material. But can poetry be ecological? Can it display or be invested with values that acknowledge the economy of interrelationship between the human and the nonhuman realms?"

Kalidasa's *Ritusamhara* doesn't merely acknowledge the interrelationship between humans and nonhuman realms, but goes beyond it in underlining the vital role the flora and fauna play in shaping human culture and civilization and how in their absence we humans would be reduced to nothing but machines.

Forrest Gander further adds—"less interested in 'nature poetry'—where nature features as theme—than in poetry that investigates—both thematically and formally—the relationship between nature and culture, language and perception."

Kalidasa's genius lies in bringing together ecological and sensual to create sensual ecopoetry of everlasting relevance. *Ritusamhara* highlights this fundamental connection between seasons and sensuality. As we face the triple threat of climate change, biodiversity loss and environmental pollution owing to our ever growing greed and culture of consumerism, we face the challenge of losing what makes us human. It is in these unprecedented times, reading and re-reading Kalidasa's *Ritusamhara* becomes essential.

– Abhay K.

SUMMER

प्रचण्डसूर्यः स्पृहणीयचन्द्रमाः
सदावगाहक्षतवारिसञ्चयः।
दिनान्तरम्योऽभ्युपशान्तमन्मथो
निदाघकालोऽयम् उपागत प्रिये।। १-१

The savage sun is ablaze, one thirsts to plunge
again and again in deep swimming pools,
the moon alone brings relief at the day's end.
Manmatha, the love-god, is tranquil,
it's just the beginning of summer, my love! 1-1

निशाः शशाङ्कक्षतनीलराजयः
क्व चिद् विचित्रं जलयन्त्रमन्दिरम् ।
मणिप्रकाराः सरसं च चन्दनं
शुचौ प्रिये यान्ति जनस्य सेव्यताम्।। १-२

After the moon has scattered darkness,
people wearing jewels and sandal creams
seek relief somewhere
at places with cool water fountains
on such summer nights, my love. 1-2

सुवासितं हर्म्यतलं मनोहरं
प्रियामुखोच्छ्वासविकम्पितं मधु।
सुतन्त्रिगीतं मदनस्य दीपनं
शुचौ निशीथेऽनुभवन्ति कामिनः।। १-३

The palace terraces fragrant with flowers,
wine quivering beneath the breath and lips
of women, sweet songs accompanied
with lutes and lyres, kindle luminous love
of amorous men at midnight, my love. 1-3

नितम्बबिम्बैः सुदुकूलमेखलैः
स्तनैः सहाराभरणैः सचन्दनैः ।
शिरोरुहैः स्नानकषायवासितैः
स्त्रियो निदाघं शमयन्ति कामिनाम्।। १-४

Round hips, their beauty augmented
with soft silk and jeweled belts,
their sandal pasted breasts shining
with strings of pearls, hair fragrant
with subtle and lingering perfumes,
women soothe the senses of their lovers
with these in the scorching summer. 1-4

नितान्तलाक्षारसरागरञ्जितैर्
नितम्बिनीनाम् चरणैः सनूपुरैः।
पदे पदे हंसरुतानुकारिभिर्
जनस्य चित्तम् क्रियते समन्मथम्।। १-५

Women with curvaceous hips, their feet coloured
bright red with laksha sap, their tinkling anklets
mimicking the sonorous crying of Hamsas,
stir desire in the hearts of young men. 1-5

Laksha: Lac
Hamsas: Swans

पयोधराश् चन्दनपङ्कचर्वितास्
तुषारगौरार्पितहारशेखराः।
नितम्बदेशाश् च सहेममेखलाः
प्रकुर्वते कस्य मनो न सोत्सुकम्।। १-६

Breasts painted with liquid sandal paste,
adorned with strings of snow-white pearls
and round hips embellished with golden girdles,
who can remain indifferent to these
and not be filled with restless longing. 1-6

समुद्गतस्वेदजिताङ्गसन्धयो
विमुच्य वासांसि गुरूणि साम्प्रतम्।
स्तनेषु तन्वंशुकम् उन्नतस्तना
निवेशयन्ति प्रमदाः सयौवनाः।। १-७

Young girls, proud and blooming,
beads of sweat shining on their perfect
bodies, take off their fancy garments
and cover their high and pointed
bosoms with thin linen stoles. 1-7

सचन्दनाम्बुव्यजनोद्भवानिलैः
सहारयष्टिस्तनमण्डलार्पितैः ।
सवल्लकीकाकलिगीतनिःस्वनैः
प्रबुध्यतेविबोध्यते सुप्त इवाद्य मन्मथः।। १-८

Gentle breeze from the fans moistened with sandal water,
soft melodious music from Vallaki lutes and Kakali pipes,
the soft press of round breasts adorned with pearl strings
awaken Manmatha, the love-god, from his deep slumber. 1-8

सितेषु हर्म्येषु निशासु योषिताम्
सुखप्रसुप्तानि मुख्यानि चन्द्रमाः।
विलोक्य नूनम् भृशम् उत्सुकश्चौरम्
निशाक्षये याति ह्रियेव पाण्डुताम्।। १-९

All night the moon looks longingly
at the faces of seductive women
sleeping on gleaming palace terraces, and
turns pale at dawn, ashamed of his guilt. 1-9

असह्यवातोद्धतरेणुमण्डला
प्रचण्डसूर्यातपतापितामही।
न शक्यते द्रष्टुमपि प्रवासिभिः
प्रियावियोगानलदग्धमानसैः।। १-१०

Earth burning with fierce heat of the Sun,
covered with dust storm raised by insufferable wind,
the lonely traveller's heart scorched with separation,
his vision blurred, weary, he can barely walk or see. 1-10

मृगाः प्रचण्डातपतापिता भृशं
तृषा महत्या परिशुष्कतालवः।
वनान्तरे तोयमिति प्रधाविता
निरीक्ष्य भिन्नाञ्जनसंनिभं नभः।। १-११

Antelopes unable to bear the sun's blinding glare,
with parched throats and tongues, rush towards
the kohl like dark clouds, mistaking a mirage
for a pool of water in another jungle. 1-11

सविभ्रमैः सस्मितजिह्मवीक्षितैर्
विलासवत्या मनसि प्रवासिनाम्।
अनङ्गसन्दीपनम् आशु कुर्वते
यथा प्रदोषाः शशिचारुभूषणाः॥ १-१२

Amorous women flirting with their
playful moves, subtle smiles, stolen glances,
and lowered eyes, ignite flames of love
in the hearts of tired travellers like a lovely evening
lit up by the glistening moon. 1-12

रवेर्मयूखैरभितापितोभृशम्
विदह्यमानः पथि सप्तपांसुभिः।
अवाङ्मुखोजिह्मगतिश्र्वसन् मुहुः
फणी मयूरस्य तले निषीदति।। १-१३

Scorched by the sun's savage rays
tormented by dust, the cobra pants
time and again with his hood drooping
as he creeps to rest in the peacock's shadow. 1-13

तृषामहत्या हतविक्रमोद्यमः
श्वसन्मुहुर्दूरविदारिताननः।
न हन्त्यदूरेऽपि गजान् मृगेश्वरो
विलोलजिह्वश्चलिताग्रकेसरः।। १-१४

Lion, the lord of beasts, lolls his tongue,
pants loudly, his jaws wide-open, mane
shaking, powerless with intense thirst,
he ignores the elephant nearby. 1-14

विशुष्ककण्ठाहृतसीकराम्भसो
गभस्तिभिर् भानुमतोऽनुतापिताः।
प्रवृद्धतृष्णोपहता जलार्थिनो न
दन्तिनाः केसरिणोऽपि बिभ्यति।। १-१५

Elephants spray cool water left in their trunks
to soothe themselves from the scorching sun,
suffering from intense thirst, they roam
searching for water, unafraid of lions anymore. 1-15

हुताग्निकल्पैः सवितुर्गभस्तिभिः
कलापिनः क्लान्तशरीरचेतसाः।
न भोगिनम् घ्नन्ति समीपवर्तिनम्
कलापचक्रेषु निवेशिताननम्।। १-१६

Peacocks, their bodies and souls wilting under the sun's
piercing rays like the flames of sacred ritual fire,
wedge their heads into the discs of their dazzling plumes
and do not kill the serpents slithering nearby. 1-16

सभद्रमुस्तम् परिशुष्ककर्दमम्
सरा: खनन् आयतपोतृमण्डलै:।
रवेर्मयूखैरभितापितो भृशम्
वराहयूथो विशतीव भूतलम्।। १-१७

Though the mud has dried up in the pond
Bhadramusta grass still thrives there, and
the wild boars scorched by the sun rays
dig deep with their long, round snouts
as if reaching out for the Earth's interior. 1-17

Bhadramusta: A kind of fragrant grass

विवस्वता तीक्ष्णतरांशुमालिना
सपङ्कतोयात् सरसोऽभितापिता:।
उत्प्लुत्य भेकस्तृषितस्य भोगिना:
फणातपत्रस्य तले निषीदति।। १-१८

Singed by the scorching sun rays
frogs leap out of the muddy marsh
and sit under the hood parasol
of a tired and thirsty cobra. 1-18

समुद्धृताशेषमृणालजालकम्
विपन्नमीनम् द्रुतभीतसारसम्।
परस्परोतुत्पीडन संहतैर्गजैः
कृतम् सरः सान्द्रविमर्दकर्दमम्।। १-१९

The tall, slender lotus-stems trampled,
the fish doomed, terrified Sarus fleeing,
the clear lake is but a sea of mud invaded
by a packed herd of jostling elephants. 1-19

Sarus crane: A large crane found in parts of the Indian subcontinent

रविप्रभोद्भिन्नशिरोमणिप्रभः
विलोलजिह्वाद्वयलीढमारुतः।
विषाग्निसूर्यातपतापिताः फणी
न हन्ति मण्डूककुलम् तृषाकुलः।। १-२०

A thirsty cobra lolls out his forked tongue
to suck the breeze, his hood shines like a jewel
under the blazing sun, tormented by his own venom,
sweltering heat and thirst, he does not hunt the frogs. 1-20

सफेनलोलायतवक्त्रसंपुटम्
विनि:सृतालोहितजिह्वमुन्मुखम्।
तृषाकुलम् नि:सृतम् अद्रिगह्वराद्
अवेक्ष्यमाणम् महिषीकुलम् जलम्।। १-२१

With foaming mouths and rose tongues
wild buffaloes emerge from the hill caverns,
frenzied by thirst, their vision blurred,
snouts raised in the air, sniffing water. 1-21

पटुतरदवदाहोच्चुष्कसस्यप्ररोहा:
परुषपवनवेगोत्क्षिप्तसंशुष्कपर्णा:।
दिनकरपरितापक्षीणतोया: समन्ताद्
विदधति भयम् उच्चौर् वीक्ष्यमाणा वनान्ता:।। १-२२

Wildfire burns the shrivelled stems of crops,
violent wind uproots their wilted straws,
sun's burning breath drains all the water,
horror reigns from the highlands to the woods. 1-22

श्वसिति विहगवर्गः शीर्णपर्णद्रुमस्थः
कपिकुलमुपयाति क्लान्तमद्रेर्निकुञ्जम्।
भ्रमति गवययूथः सर्वतस्तोयमिच्छञ्
शरभकुलमजिह्मं प्रोद्धरत्यम्बुकूपात्।। १-२३

A flock of panting birds perches on the leafless tree,
a tribe of tired monkeys seeks shelter in the hill cavern,
a herd of wild buffaloes wanders uneasily, seeking water,
Sarabhas briskly drink whatever water is left in the lakes. 1-23

Sarabha: A part lion and part bird creature in Hindu mythology which is also sometimes described as an eight-legged deer

विकचनवकुसुम्भस्वच्छसिन्दूरभासा
प्रबलपवनवेगोद्धूतवेगेन तूर्णम् ।
तरुविटपलताग्रालिंगनव्याकुलेनदिशि
दिशि परिदग्धा भूमयः पावकेन।। १-२४

Wildfire like freshly blossomed bright ochre safflower
aided by the violent gusts of wind embraces eagerly
the creepers and tree tops on the banks of the rivers
and lakes, burning every quarter of the earth quickly. 1-24

ज्वलति पवन वृद्धः पर्वतानाम् दरीषु
स्फुटति पटु निनादैः शुष्कवंशस्थलीषु।
प्रसरति तृण मध्ये लब्ध वृद्धिः क्षणेन
ग्लपयति मृगवर्गम् प्रांत लग्नो दवाग्नि।। १-२५

Wildfire blazing the mountain valleys
intensified by violent winds, sweeps
through the tall groves of dry bamboo
which shatter instantly with crackling sounds,
and fueled further spreads to straw fields
scarring the herds of forest deer. 1-25

बहुतर इव जातः शाल्मलीनाम् वनेषु
स्फुरति कनकगौरः कोटरेषु द्रुमाणाम्।
परिणतदलशाखानुत्पतन् प्रांशुवृक्षान्
भ्रमति पवनधूतः सर्वतोऽग्निर् वनान्ते।। १-२६

The forest fire goes wild in the groves of Salmali trees
whose empty trunks on fire glow like glazed gold,
leaping from tree to tree, robbing their dry leaves,
invading the forest's heart abetted by the delinquent wind. 1-26

Salmali: Silk-cotton

गजगवयमृगेन्द्रा वह्निसंतप्तदेहाः
सुहृद इव समेता द्वन्द्वभावं विहाय ।
हुतवहपरिखेदादाशु निर्गत्य कक्षाद्
विपुलपुलिनदेशां निम्नगां संविशंति॥ १-२७

Lions, elephants, buffaloes, their bodies
scorched by fire, flee the forest
and rest on the broad sandy banks of the river,
like friends, putting aside their enmity. 1-27

कमलवनचिताम्बुः पाटलामोदरम्यः
सुखसलिलनिषेकः सेव्यचन्द्रांशुहारः।
व्रजतु तव निदाघः कामिनीभिः समेतो
निशि सुललितगीते हर्म्यपृष्ठे सुखेन।। १-२८

Blooming lotuses in the ponds, refreshing Patala flowers,
pleasant waters in the pools, soothing moonbeams,
may this season of summer be spent in the company
of charming women on the rooftops, with music and song! 1-28

Patala: Trumpet flower or Bignonia sauveolens

RAINS

सशीरकाम्भोधरमत्तकुञ्जरस्
तटित्पताकोऽशनिशब्दमर्दलः।
समागतो राजवत् उद्धतद्युतिर्
घनागमः कामिजनप्रियः प्रिये।। २-१

The season of rains approaches, my love, like a king,
his royal cavalcade in full ceremonial procession,
dark clouds—his war elephants in their rutting season,
glowing flashes of lightning—his tapering victory flag,
and roaring thunder—the sound of beating war drums
welcomed by the crowd of lovers with maddening cheers. 2-1

नितान्तनीलोत्पलपत्रकान्तिभिः
क्वचित् प्रभिन्नाञ्जनराशिसन्निभैः।
क्वचित् सगर्भप्रमदास्तनप्रभैः
समाचितम् व्योम धनैः समन्ततः।। २-२

The sky is overcast with dark clouds all around
glowing deeply like the petals of dark blue lotuses,
somewhere dark like heaps of black kohl,
elsewhere like the dark nipples of pregnant women. 2-2

तृषाकुलैश्चातकपक्षिणाम् कुलैः
प्रयाचितास् तोयभरावलम्बिनः।
प्रयान्ति मन्दम् बहुधारवर्षिणो
बलाहकाः श्रोत्रमनोहरस्वनाः।। २-३

Taking pity on prayers of thirsty Chatakas,
the rain bearing clouds hang low and go slow,
pouring generous showers, the ceaseless
tapping of rain sounds sweet to the ears. 2-3

Chatakas: A slender, long-tailed, crested black and white cuckoo which quenches its thirst from rain drops

बलाहकश्चाशनिशब्दमर्दला:
सुरेन्द्रचापम् दधतस् तडिद्गुणम्।
सुतीक्ष्णधारापतनोग्रसायकैस्
तुदन्ति चेत: प्रसभम् प्रवासिनाम।। २-४

Clouds thunder like beating drums,
rainbow arches across the sky and
using lightning as its string hurls sharp arrows
of rains assailing the minds of lonely travellers. 2-4

प्रभिन्नवैदूर्यनिभैस् तृणाङ्कुरैः
समाचिताप्रोत्थितकन्दलीदलैः।
विभाति शुक्लेतररत्नभूषिता।
वाराङ्गनेव क्षितिर् इन्द्रगोपकैः।। २-५

Like jade fragments, the green grass rises
spreading its blades to catch raindrops,
red Indragopaka insects perch on fresh
leaf-buds bursting forth from the Kandali plants
the earth smiles like an elegant lady
draped in nature's colourful jewels. 2-5

Kandali: Banana
Indragopaka: An insect

सदा मनोज्ञम् स्वनदुत्सवोत्सुकं
विकीर्णविस्तीर्णकलापशोभितम्।
ससम्भ्रमालिङ्गनचुम्बनाकुलं
प्रवृत्तनृत्यम् कुलम् अद्य बर्हिणाम्।। २-६

Roused by the pleasing sound of thundering clouds
amorous peacocks fill the air with their joyous cries
welcoming the rain, throwing themselves into love-play
—billing and cooing, and begin to dance
spreading out their resplendent feathers. 2-6

निपातयन्त्यः परितस् तटद्रुमान्
प्रवृद्धवेगैः सलिलैर् अनिर्मलैः।
स्त्रियः सुदुष्टा इव जातिविभ्रमाः
प्रयान्ति नद्यस् त्वरितम् पयोनिधिम्।। २-७

Swollen rivers surging with currents of muddy waters
rush to meet the sea, uprooting the trees on their banks,
so do the lascivious women splatter their men with dirt
and rush to meet their lovers to quench their wild desires. 2-7

तृणोत्करैर् उद्गतकोमलाङ्कुरैर्
विचित्रनीलहरिणीमुखक्षतैः।
वनानि वैन्ध्यानि हरन्ति मानसं
विभूषितान्य् उद्गतपल्लवैर् दृशैः।। २-८

The slopes of Vindhya lush with tender grass
grazed delightfully by the gentle does,
and the woods full of blooming trees
dressed in new leaves, steal the hearts. 2-8

विलोलनेत्रोत्पलशोभिताननैर्
मृगैः समन्ताद् उपजातसाध्वसैः।
समाचिता सैकतिनी वनस्थली
समुत्सुकत्वम् प्रकरोति चेतसः।। २-९

The forest glades and meadows
are overcrowded with herds of startled deer
whose eyes quiver like the freshly bloomed
dark-blue Utpala, pleasing the mind. 2-9

Utpala: Blue lotus

अभीक्ष्णम् उच्चौर् ध्वनता पयोमुचा
घनान्धकारीकृतशर्वरीष्व् अपि।
तडित्प्रभादर्शितमार्गभूमयः
प्रयान्ति रागाद् अभिसारिका: स्त्रियः।। २-१०

Even in the pitch-dark, somber, cloudy nights
braving the rains and thunder, pleasure-seeking
women head for their mid-night rendezvous
with flashes of lightning guiding their way. 2-10

पयोधरैर् भीमगभीरनिःस्वनैस्
तडिद्भिर् उद्वेजितचेतसो भृशम्।
कृतापराधान् अपि योषितः प्रियान्
परिष्वजन्ते शयने निरन्तरम्।। २-११

Bursts of lightning and thunder terrify
young women who get cozy with their
lovers in the bed, full of desire, forgiving
and forgetting their past philandering. 2-11

विलोचनेन्दीवरवारिबिन्दुभिर्
निषिक्तबिम्बाधरचारुपल्लवाः।
निरस्तमाल्याभरणानुलेपनाः
स्थिता निराशाः प्रमदाः प्रवासिनाम्।। २-१२

The beloveds of the travellers, waiting for them
to get home, discard flowers, jewels and cosmetics,
in despair, tear-drops falling from their lotus-eyes,
like dew-drops, moistening their leaf like tender lips,
which are bright red like the ripe bimba fruits. 2-12

Bimba: Ivy gourd to which lips of women are often compared

विपाण्डुरम् कीटरजस्तृणान्वितम्
भुजङ्गवद् वक्रगतिप्रसर्पितम्।
ससाध्वसैर् भेककुलैर् निरीक्षितम्
प्रयाति निम्नाभिमुखम् नवोदकम्।। २-१३

Fresh water turns murky mixing
with mud, grass and insects, and
rushes down the slope sinuously like a serpent,
frogs watching it with great trepidation. 2-13

विपत्रपुष्पाम् नलिनीम् समुत्सुका
विहाय भृङ्गाः श्रुतिहारिनिःस्वनाः।
पतन्ति मूढाः शिखिनाम् प्रनृत्यतां
कलापचक्रेषु नवोत्पलाशया।। २-१४

Confused bees leave the lotuses
which have shed their petals
and rush to the dancing peacocks
circling over the discs of their plumes,
mistaking them for new lotuses in bloom. 2-14

वनद्विपानाम् नववारिदस्वनैर्
मदान्वितानाम् ध्वनताम् मुहुर् मुहुः।
कपोलदेशा विमलोत्पलप्रभाः
सभृङ्गयूथैर् मदवारिभिश् चिता।। २-१५

Wild rutting elephants trumpet incessantly
as if challenging the thundering clouds,
their secreting temples resemble dark blue lotuses
and are frequented by hosts of honey bees. 2-15

सितोत्पलाभाम्बुदचुम्बितोपलाः
समाचिताः प्रस्रवणैः समन्ततः।
प्रवृत्तनृत्यैः शिखिभिः समाकुलाः
समुत्सुकत्वम् जनयन्ति भूधराः।। २-१६

Clouds, like shining silver lotuses,
kissing the peaks of the mountains,
cascades, creeks and ravines
overflowing with gurgling water,
earth alive with dancing peacocks,
these create a carnival of visual delights. 2-16

कदम्बसर्जार्जुनकेतकीवनं
विकम्पयंस् तत्कुसुमाधिवासिनः।
समीकराभोधरसङ्गशीतलः
समीरणः कम् न करोति सोत्सुकम्।। २-१७

Winds fragrant from merrily fondling the blossoms
of Kadamba, Sarja, Ketaki and Arjuna, cool
after consorting the clouds and rain drops,
how can these not fill the heart with ecstasy? 2-17

Kadamba: Neolamarckia cadamba, with English common names burflower-tree, laran, and Leichhardt pine, and called kadam locally, is an evergreen, tropical tree native to South Asia

Sarja: Sal tree, a sacred tree in Hindu mythology, native to South Asia

Ketaki: Fragrant screw-pine

Arjuna: Arjun tree

शिरोरुहैः श्रोणितटावलम्बिभिः
कृतावतंसैः कुसुमैः सुगन्धिभिः।
स्तनैः सहारैर् वदनैः ससीधुभिः
स्त्रियो रतिम् सञ्जनयन्ति कामिनाम्।। २-१८

Women with long hair touching their hips,
fragrant flowers behind their ears, pearl strings
caressing their breasts, their lips drunk on
wine, whet the desire of their lovers. 2-18

तटिल्लताशक्रधनुर्विभूषिताः
पयोधरास् तोयभरावलम्बिनः।
स्त्रियश् च काञ्चीमणिकुण्डलोज्ज्वला
हरन्ति चेतो युगपत् प्रवासिनाम्।। २-१९

The low hanging rain clouds with their lightning
and vibrant rainbow hues, and women
with their glittering girdles and gem earrings,
both entice the heart of the lonely travellers. 2-19

माला: कदम्बनवकेसरकेतकीभिर्
आयोजिता: शिरसि बिभ्रति योषितोऽद्य।
कर्णान्तरेषु ककुभद्रुममञ्जरीभिर्
इच्चानुकूलरचितान् अवतंसकांश् च।। २-२०

Women crown their heads with diadems
woven from freshly bloomed Kadamba,
Kesara and Ketaki flowers, make various
ornaments of choice with Kakubha tassels
and also wear them as earrings. 2-20

Kakubḥa: Arjun tree

कालागुरुप्रचुरचन्दनचर्चिताङ्ग्यः
पुष्पावतंससुरभीकृतकेशपाशाः।
श्रुत्वा ध्वनिम् जलमुचाम् त्वरितम् प्रदोषं
शय्यागृहम् गुरुगृहात् प्रदिशन्ति नार्यः।। २-२१

Newlywed brides anointed with sandal paste
and perfumed with kalaguru, wearing earrings
of flowers which render fragrance to their plaited hair,
hearing the clouds thunder at dusk, slip away
from their elders into their bedchambers. 2-21

Kalaguru: Black Agarwood or Aloeswood

कुवलयदलनीलैर् उन्नतैस् तोयनम्रैर्
मृदुपवनैर् मन्दमन्दम् चलद्भिः।
अपहृतम् इव चेतस् तोयदैः सेन्द्रचापैः
पथिकजनवधूनाम् तद्वियोगाकुलानाम्।। २-२२

Dark clouds, like dark blue lotus petals,
hanging low, laden with water, move slowly
driven by gentle breeze, gleaming with rainbows,
luring the hearts of lonely wives of the wayfarers
who are restless because of separation. 2-22

मुदित इव कदम्बैर् जातिपुष्पैः समन्तात्
पवनचलितशाखैः शाखिभिर् नृत्यतीव।
हसितम् इव विधत्ते सूचिभिः केतकीनां
नवसलिलनिषेकच्छिन्नतापो वनान्तः।। २-२३

Fresh rain showers cool the simmering forest,
joyous, it bursts with Kadamba blossoms,
dances happily—tree branches swaying
with playful winds—and appears to smile
through sharp white needles of Ketaki. 2-23

शिरसि बकुलमालाम् मालतीभिः समेतां
विकसितनवपुष्पैर् यूथिकाकुड्मलैश् च।
विकचनवकदम्बैः कर्णपूरम् वधूनां
रचयति जलदौघः कान्तवत् काल एषः।। २-२४

The season with its cluster of rain clouds
is like a lover adorning the hair of young women
with Bakula and Malati flowers and making
new trinkets for their ears from Yuthika buds
and freshly blossomed Kadamba flowers. 2-24

Bakula: Spanish cherry or bullet wood, its fruit and bark are used in Ayurvedic medicine

Malati: Native to India, Malati is a big, woody climber which bears clusters of fragrant, white, jasmine like flowers

Yuthika: Yuthika is a beautiful Jasmine vine with fragrant, attractive white flowers

दधति वरकुचाग्रैर् उन्नतैर् हारयष्टिं
प्रतनुसितदुकूलान्यायतैः श्रोणिबिम्बैः।
नवजलकणसेकाद् उद्गताग् रोमराजीं
ललितवलिविभङ्गैर् मध्यदेशैश् च नार्यः।। २-२५

Young women wear pearl-strings
on their ample breasts, thin white linen
on their round hips, delicate waist-folds
adorn the middle of their bodies, and
fine hair on their bellies bristle
upon the touch of cool rain drops. 2-25

नवजलकणसङ्गाच्छीततामादधानः
कुसुमभरनतानाम् लासकः पादपानाम्।
जनितरुचिरगन्धः केतकीनाम् रजोभिः
परिहरति नभस्वान् प्रोषितानाम् मनांसि।। २-२६

The flower laden trees, drunk on fresh rains,
sway and dance with the wind, which turns
fragrant upon touching Ketaki's golden pollens
and steals the heart of the lonely travellers. 2-26

जलधरविनतानाम् आशरयोऽस्माकम् उच्चिर्
अयम् इति जलसेकैस् तोयदास् तोयनम्राः।
अतिशयपरुषाभिर ग्रीष्मवह्नेः शिलाभिः
समुपजनिततापम् ह्लादयन्तीव विन्ध्यम्।। २-२७

The rain clouds hang low with the weight of water,
and taking the Vindhyas to be their highest resting place
bless the mountains engulfed in severe summer fires,
with heavy rain showers, as though appeasing them. 2-27

बहुगुणरमणीयः कामिनीचित्तहारी
तरुविटपलतानाम् बान्धवो निर्विकारः।
जलदसमय एव प्राणिनाम् प्राणभूतो
दिशतु तव हितानि प्रायशो वाञ्छितानि।। २-२८

May this season of rains, full of delights,
stealing hearts of amorous women, a formless
friend of trees, creepers and shrubs, and the life-spirit
of all living beings, grant your deepest desires! 2-28

AUTUMN

काशांशुका विकचपद्ममनोज्ञवक्त्रा
सोन्मादहंसरवनूपुरनादरम्या।
आपक्वशालिरुचिरा तनुगात्रयष्टिः
प्राप्ता शरन्नववधूरिव रूपरम्या।। ३-१

Here comes autumn dressed in silver Kasa blossoms,
blooming white lotus—her pretty face,
rapturous cries of wild geese—tinkling of her anklet bells,
ripening rice sheaves bending with breeze—her graceful form.
Look, the autumn has arrived like a charming bride! 3-1

काशैर्मही शिशिरदीधितिना रजन्यो
हंसैर् जलानि सरिताम् कुमुदैः सरांसि।
सप्तच्च्दैः कुसुमभारनतैर् वनान्ताः
शुक्लीकृतान्य् उपवनानि च मालतीभिः।। ३-२

The earth wrapped in white Kasa blossoms,
nights lit up with the silver moon,
river currents white with Hamsas
and ponds filled with white lilies,
forests teeming with Saptachadda plants
bowing gently with the weight of their flowers,
gardens fragrant with white Malati blossoms,
white reigns all around, pleasing the eyes. 3-2

Kasa: Saccharum spontaneum (wild sugarcane)
Saptachadda: Seven leaved banana plants

चञ्चन्मनोज्ञशफरीरसनाकलापा:
पर्यन्तसंस्थितसिताण्डजपङ्क्तिहारा:।
नद्यो विशालपुलिनान्तनितम्बबिम्बा
मन्दम् प्रयान्ति समदा: प्रमदा इवाद्य।। ३-३

The clear streams move gently like proud women,
becoming calm with their soft and unhurried steps,
leaping, glittering fish—girdles around their waists,
white swans—pearl necklaces around their bosoms,
and the broad sandy banks—their curved hips. 3-3

व्योम क्वचिद् रजतशङ्खमृणालगौरैस्
त्यक्ताम्बुभिर् लघुतया शतशः प्रयातैः।
संलक्ष्यते पवनवेगचलैः पयोदै
राजेव चामरवरैर् उपवीज्यमानः।। ३-४

Having shed the rain, swayed by the wind
clouds are splintered into hundreds of cloudlets
and shine like silver conch shells at places,
at others, they are pale like lotus stalks.
The sky appears stately like a king
fanned gently by the royal chowries. 3-4

भिन्नाञ्जनप्रचयकान्ति नभो मनोज्ञं
बन्धूकपुष्परचितारुणता च भूमिः।
वप्राश् च चारु कमलावृतभूमिभागाः
प्रोत्कण्ठयन्ति न मनो भुवि कस्य युतः।। ३–५

The sky looks dark blue like glossy kohl,
the earth is glowing like dawn, tinged
with pink by Bandhuka pollen, far fields
and ravines are full of blooming lotuses,
whose heart would not throb
with sensuous longing seeing all these? 3-5

Bandhuka: Jungle geranium, Ixora Coccinea

मन्दानिलाकुलितचारुतराग्रशाखः
पुष्पोद्गमप्रचयकोमलपल्लवाग्रः।
मत्तद्विरेफपरिपीतमधुप्रसेकश्
चित्तम् विसारयति कस्य न कोविदारः।। ३-६

The gentle breeze caresses the flower buds
and tender leaves on swaying boughs,
the delirious bees drink greedily
honey trickling from Kovidara trees,
whose heart would not overflow with joy
looking at these sceneries? 3-6

Kovidara: Mountain ebony, Bauhinia, Kachnar

तारागणप्रवरभूषणम् उद्वहन्ती
मेघावरोधपरिमुक्तशशाङ्कवक्त्रा।
ज्योत्स्नादुकूलम् अमलम् रजनी दधाना
वृद्धिम् प्रयात्य् अनुदिनम् प्रमदेव बाला।। ३-७

The autumn night, dressed in moonlight,
glistening—the veil of clouds gone,
myriad stars—her gleaming jewels,
resembles a moon-faced adolescent
turning gracefully into a charming bride. 3-7

कारण्डवाननविघट्टितवीचिमाला:
कादम्बसारसचयाकुलतीरदेशा:।
कुर्वन्ति हंसविरुतै: परितो जनस्य
प्रीतिम् सरोरुहरजोऽरुणितास् तटिन्य:।। ३-८

Wild ducks pecking at water ripples,
river banks alive with the cries
of jostling Kalahamsa and Sarus cranes,
streams reddened with red pollen grains
and lotuses, these delight people's heart. 3-8

Kalahamsa: Black Swan

नेत्रोत्सवो हृदयहारिमरीचिमालः
प्रह्लादकः शिशिरसीकरवारिवर्षी।
पत्युर् वियोगविषदिग्धशरक्षतानां
चन्द्रो वहत्य् अतितराम् तनुम् अङ्गनानाम्।। ३-९

The moon delights the eyes,
ravishes the hearts with its cool light,
yet its cold beams, pierce like poison arrows,
the delicate bodies of charming women
separated from their lovers. 3-9

आकम्पयन् फलभरानतशालिजालान्
आनर्तयंस् तरुवरान् कुसुमावनम्रान्।
उत्फुल्लपङ्कजवनाम् नलिनीम् विधुन्वन्
यूनांमनश् चलयति प्रसभम् नभस्वान्।। ३-१०

The breeze sways and bends the paddy crop,
rushes to tree tops laden with flowers,
making them dance, and seductively strokes
the fully blossomed lotuses in the ponds,
fervently arousing the minds of the young. 3-10

सोन्मादहंसमिथुनैर् उपशोभितानि
स्वच्चप्रफुल्लकमलोत्पलभूषितानि।
मन्दप्रभातपवनोद्गतवीचिमालान्य्
उत्कण्ठयन्ति सहसा हृदयम् सरांसि।। ३-११

The lakes, wearing the necklace of ripples
dancing with the morning breeze,
filled with blossoming lotuses and indigo lilies,
adorned with a pair of Hamsas longing for each other,
fill the heart with amorous desires. 3-11

नष्टम् धनुर्बलभिदो जलदोदरेषु
सौदामिनी स्फुरति नाद्य वियत्पताका।
धुन्वन्ति पक्षपवनैर् न नभो बलाका:
पश्यन्ति नोन्नतमुखा गगनम् मयूरा:।। ३-१२

Rainbows have vanished into the belly of the clouds,
lightnings—the sky flags, do not flash anymore,
cranes do not flap their wings any longer displacing
the air, and peacocks no longer look towards the sky
with their raised heads. 3-12

नृत्यप्रयोगरहिताञ् चिखिनो विहाय
हंसान् उपैति मदनो मधुरप्रगीतान्।
मुक्त्वा कदम्बकुटजार्जुनसर्जनीपान्
सप्तच्चदानुपगता कुसुमोद्गमश्रीः।। ३-१३

Love-god graces the swans, who sing
softly, sweetly, abandoning the peacocks,
who don't dance anymore, and the splendour
of blossom deserting Kutaja, Kadamba, Arjuna,
Sarja and Nipa, now blesses the Saptachadda. 3-13

Kutaja: Holarrhena pubescens, a flowering plant with medicinal properties

Nipa: A flower that blossoms in the rainy season

शेफालिकाकुसुमगन्धमनोहराणि
स्वस्थस्थिताण्डजकुलप्रतिनाद् इतानि।
पर्यन्तसस्थितमृगीनयनोत्पलानि
प्रोत्कण्ठयन्त्य् उप्वनानि मनांसि पुंसाम्।। ३-१४

The woodlands, perfumed with Sephalika blossoms,
exuberant with the songs of twittering birds,
lotus-eyed gazelles roaming freely in the glades,
light the fire of longing in the young hearts. 3-14

Sephalika: A tree that bears six-petalled flowers

कह्लारपद्मकुमुदानि मुहुर् विधुन्वंस्
तत्सङ्गमाद् अधिकशीतलताम् उपेतः।
उत्कण्ठयत्य् अतितराम् पवनः प्रभाते
पत्रान्तलग्नतुहिनाम्बुविधूयमानः।। ३-१५

Caressing the Padma, Kalhara, and Kumuda,
the morning breeze, cooled by the dew-drops
clinging to the tips of their leaves,
grows even more pleasant and exhilirating. 3-15

Padma, Kalhara, Kumada: Different varieties of lotuses

सम्पन्नशालिनिचयावृतभूतलानि
स्वस्थस्थितप्रचुरगोकुलशोभितानि।
हंसैः ससारसकुलैः प्रतिनादितानि
सीमान्तराणि जनयन्ति नृणाम् प्रमोदम्।। ३-१६

The fields full of ripened paddy, adorned
with herds of healthy cattle—flourishing,
the horizon reverberating with pleasant cries
of Sarus and Hamsa, fill people's heart with joy. 3-16

हंसैर् जिता सुललिता गतिर् अङ्गनानाम्
अम्भोरुहैर् विकसितैर् मुखचन्द्रकान्तिः।
नीलोत्पलैर् मदकलानि विलोकितानि
भ्रूविभ्रमाश् च रुचिरास् तनुभिस् तरङ्गैः।। ३-१७

The swan's moves outrival the steps
of the most lissom women,
fully blossomed silver lotuses
outrival the glow of their moon like faces,
the sway of bright blue lilies outrival
their sidelong amorous glances,
and the gentle ripples in the clear pools of water
outrival the fluttering of their eyelashes. 3-17

श्यामा लताः कुसुमभारनतप्रवाला
स्त्रीणाम् हरन्ति घृतभूषणबाहुकान्तिम्।
दन्तावभाविशदस्मितचन्द्रकान्तिं
कङ्केलिपुष्परुचिरा नवमालती च।। ३-१८

The Shyamaa creepers' twigs full of flowers
outrival the grace of women's jeweled arms
and delightful Malati blossoms and Asoka flowers
steal the splendour of radiant smiles of women. 3-18

Shyamaa: Black creeper

Asoka or Saraca asoca is considered a sacred tree by the Hindus and is also associated with Kamadeva, the Hindu god of love

केशान् नितान्तघननीलविकुञ्चिताग्रान्
आपूरयन्ति वनिता नवमालतीभिः।
कर्णेषु च प्रवरकाञ्चनकुड्मलेषु
नीलोत्पलानि विविधानि निवेशयन्ति।। ३-१९

Young women adorn their curly hair,
dark as a rain cloud, with fresh Malati flowers
and wear fresh blue Utpala buds behind their ears
embellished with precious gold earrings. 3-19

हारैः सचन्दनरसैः स्तनमण्डलानि
श्रोणीतटम् सुविपुलम् रसनाकलापैः।
पादाम्बुजानि कलनूपुरशेखरैश् च
नार्यः प्रहृष्टमनसोऽद्य विभूषयन्ति।। ३-२०

Women with contented hearts
rub sandal cream on their round bosoms
and adorn them with strings of pearls,
embellish their ample hips with gold girdles,
and their lotus feet with jingling anklets. 3-20

स्फुटकुमुदचितानाम् राजहंसस्थितानां
मरकतमणिभासा वारिणा भूषितानाम्।
श्रियम् अतिशयरूपाम् व्योम तोयाशयानां
वहति विगतमेघम् चन्द्रतारावकीर्णम्।। ३-२१

The autumn sky rivals the exalted splendours of the earth
emerald hue of the sky—lakes with emerald waters
cloudless sky filled with stars—ponds abound with white lilies
and the shining moon in the clear sky—the royal swan. 3-21

शरदि कुमुदसङ्गाद् वायवो वान्ति शीता
विगतजलदवृन्दा दिग्विभागा मनोज्ञाः।
विगतकलुषम् अम्भः श्यानपङ्का धरित्री
विमलकिरणचन्द्रम् व्योम ताराविचित्रम्।। ३-२२

The star-studded autumn sky is enchanting
—the moon shining with impeccable purity,
breeze cool from caressing the white-lilies,
weather clear—the rain clouds scattered,
waters devoid of slush, earth no longer slippery. 3-22

दिवसकरमयूखैर बोध्यमानम् प्रभाते
वरयुवतिमुखाभम् पङ्कजम् जृम्भतेऽद्य।
कुमुदम् अपि गतेऽस्तम् लीयते चन्द्रबिम्बे
हसितम् इव वधूनाम् प्रोषितेषु प्रियेषु।। ३-२३

Aroused by the sun rays at sunrise,
Pankaja opens up like glowing face
of a young woman, while the moon
turns pale, smile vanishes from Kumuda
like that of the young women,
after their lovers are gone far away. 3-23

Pankaja, Kumuda: Different varieties of lotuses

अिसतनयनलक्ष्मीम् लक्षयित्वोत्पलेषु
क्वणितकनकाञ्चीम् मत्तहंसस्वनेषु।
अधररुचिरशोभाम् बन्धुजीवे प्रियाणां
पथिकजन इदानीम् रोदिति भ्रान्तचित्तः।। ३-२४

Seeing the dark eyes of his beloved
in blooming Utpala flowers, freshness
of her red lips in Bandhujiva blossoms,
hearing the tinkling bells of her golden
girdles in the sweet cries of love-mad Hamsas,
the traveler chokes in delirium. 3-24

Utpala: Blue lotus
Bandhujiva: Noon flower or Scarlet Mallow

स्त्रीणाम् विहाय वदनेषु शशाङ्कलक्ष्मीं
कामम् च हंसवचनम् मणिनूपुरेषु।
बन्धूककान्तिम् अधरेषु मनोहरेषु
कापि प्रयाति सुभगा शरदागमश्रीः।। ३-२५

The radiance of the moon is now found in the faces
of charming women, the sonorous cries of the Hamsas
in the tinkling of their gem-studded anklets,
and the deep-red glow of Bandhuka blossoms
in their luscious lips. Who knows where
the glorious autumn is departing? 3-25

विकचकमलवक्त्रा फुल्लनीलोत्पलाक्षी
विकसितनवकाशश्वेतवासो वसाना।
कुमुदरुचिरकान्तिः कामिनीवोन्मदेयं
प्रतिदिशतु शरदश् चेतसः प्रीतिम् अग्र्याम॥ ३-२६

Blossomed pink lotus as its face,
unfolded blue lilies as its eyes,
fresh white Kasa blossoms as its robe,
may this autumn, with its heart-stealing
brilliance, bring you utmost delight,
like your lustful beloved, madly in love with you! 3-26

Kasa: Saccharum spontaneum (wild sugarcane)

FROST

नवप्रवालोद्गमसस्यरम्यः
प्रफुल्लोध्रः परिपक्वशालिः।
विलीनपद्मः प्रपतत्तुषारो
हेमन्तकालः समुपागतोऽयम्।। ४-१

Barley shoots sprouting suddenly
weaving a green embroidery, paddy
ripening, Lodhra blossoms all around,
lotuses withered away, dew falling heavily,
these ring in the fine season of frost. 4-1

Lodhra: Symplocos, its powder nourishes the skin

मनोहरैः कुङ्कुमरागरक्तस्
तुषारकुन्देन्दुनिभैश् च हारैः।
विलासिनीनाम् स्तनशालिनीनाम्
अलंक्रियन्ते स्तनमण्डलानि।। ४-२

The bosoms of amorous women are
daubed with heart-stealing Kumkum,
the necklace of Kunda flowers on them
glows like dew drops and the moon. 4-2

Kumkum: Saffron from Kashmir
Kunda: Jasmine

न बाहुयुग्मेषु विलासिनीनाम्
प्रयान्ति सङ्गम् वलयाङ्गदानि।
नितम्बबिम्बेषु नवम् दुकूलम्
तन्वंशुकम् पीनपयोधरेषु।। ४-३

The cool touch of bracelets on wrists,
armlets on upper arms, and silk
on round hips and full bosoms,
is unbearable for the amorous women. 4-3

काञ्चीगुणैः काञ्चनरत्नचित्रैर्नो
भूषयन्ति प्रमदा नितम्बम्।
न नूपुरैर् हंसरुतम् भजद्भिः
पादाम्बुजान्य् अम्बुजकान्तिभाञ्जि।। ४-४

Golden girdles studded with gems
do not adorn the hips of women anymore,
nor do their lotus feet kissed by sonorous
anklets rival the sweet sounding Hamsas. 4-4

Hamsas: Cranes

गात्राणि कालीयकचर्चितानि
सपत्रलेखानि मुखाम्बुजानि।
शिरांसि कालागुरुधूपितानि
कुर्वन्ति नार्यः सुरतोत्सवाय।। ४-५

Young women rub Kalakeya perfumed powder
on their bodies and tattoo their lotus faces
with flower patterns, and perfume their hair
with the incense of Kakaguru as they get ready
for the joyous carnival of lovemaking. 4-5

Kalakeya: Fragrant turmeric powder
Kakaguru: Resins of Aloe Vera

रतिश्रमक्षामविपाण्डुवक्त्राः
सम्प्राप्तहर्षाभ्युदयास् तरुण्यः।
हसन्ति नोच्चैर् दशनाग्रभिन्नान्
प्रपीयमानान् अधरान् अवेक्ष्य।। ४-६

Though their faces are pale from weariness
after lovemaking, young women are content
with their amorous desires fulfilled,
their lower lips aching from love-bites,
they fear laughing out loud. 4-6

पीनस्तनोरःस्थलभागशोभाम्
आसाद्य तत्पीडनजातखेदः।
तृणाग्रलग्नैस् तुहिनैः पतद्भिर्
आक्रन्दतीवोषसि शीतकालः।। ४-७

Sensitive to the sensuous and full breasts
of women, disheartened to see them pressed
so hard, the season of frost cries at dawn,
shedding dewdrop-tears from the blades of grass. 4-7

प्रभूतशालिप्रसवैश्चितानि
मृगाङ्गनायूथविभूषितानि।
मनोहरक्रौञ्चनिनादितानि
सीमान्तराण्य् उत्सुकयन्ति चेतः।। ४-८

The fields covered with ripened paddy
as far as eyes can see, their boundaries
full of herd of does, midlands filled with
sweet cries of graceful demoiselle cranes.
Ah! What passion they arouse in the heart! 4-8

प्रफुल्लनीलोत्पलशोभितानि
सोन्मादकादम्बविभूषितानि।
प्रसन्नतोयानि सुशीतलानि
सरांसि चेतांसि हरन्ति पुंसाम्।। ४-९

Fully blossomed blue lotuses adorning
the lakes, and passionate Kalahamsas
courting in the crystal-clear, chilly
waters, captivate everyone's heart. 4-9

Kalahamsas: Black swans

पाकम् व्रजन्ति हिमजातशीतैर्
आधूयमाना सततम् मरुद्भिः।
प्रिये प्रियङ्गुः प्रियविप्रयुक्ताः
विपाण्डुताम् याति विलासिनीव।। ४-१०

The Priyangu creeper has turned pale,
my love, lying exposed in freezing cold,
facing constant onslaught from the icy wind,
like ashen face of women parted from their lovers. 4-10

Priyangu: Aglaia elaeagnoidea or perfumed cherry

पुष्पासवामोदिसुगन्धिवक्त्रो
निःश्वासवातैः सुरभीकृताङ्गः।
परस्पराङ्गव्यतिरिक्तशायी
शेते जनः कामरसानुविद्धः।। ४-११

Lovers sleep entwined in each other's arms
sipping the sweet nectar of love,
their mouths perfumed with flower-wine,
their bodies covered in sweet fragrance
of their deep breath. 4-11

दन्तच्छदैः सव्रणदन्तचिह्नैः
स्तनैश्च पाण्यग्रकृताभिलेखैः।
संसूच्यते निर्दयम् अङ्गनानां
रतोपयोगो नवयौवनानाम्।। ४-१२

Women in the spring of their youth
with ruthless love bites on their lips,
and nail marks on their full breasts,
reveal passionate spells of lovemaking. 4-12

काचिद् विभूषयति दर्पणसक्तहस्ता
बालातपेषु वनिता वदनारविन्दम्।
दन्तच्चदम् प्रियतमेन निपीतसारं
दन्ताग्रभिन्नम् अवकृष्य निरीक्षते च।। ४-१३

A young woman holding a mirror in her hand
puts makeup on her face in the morning sun,
and pouting her lips—whose nectar was sucked
by her lover at night, surveys the teeth marks. 4-13

अन्या प्रकामसुरतश्रमखिन्नदेहा
रात्रिप्रजागरविपाटलनेत्रपद्मा।
स्रस्तांसदेशलुलिताकुलकेशपाशा
निद्राम् प्रयाति मृदुसूर्यकराभितप्ता।। ४-१४

Yet another woman, her body weary
after sleepless, passionate night of lovemaking,
her eyes white like lotus, hair tousled on shoulders,
falls asleep basking under the balmy sun. 4-14

निर्माल्यदाम परिमुक्तमनोज्ञगन्धं
मूर्ध्नोऽपनीय घननीलशिरोरुहान्ताः।
पीनोन्नतस्तनभरानतगात्रयष्ट्यः
कुर्वन्ति केशरचनाम् अपरास् तरुण्यः॥ ४-१५

Other young women remove faded flowers,
which have lost their fragrance, from the chaplets
worn over their dark hair resembling dense rain clouds
and busy themselves restyling their hair,
the weight of their bosoms make their slender
bodies dainty like pearl pendants, stoop slightly. 4-15

अन्या प्रियेण परिभुक्तमवेक्ष्य गात्रं
हर्षान्विता विरचिताधरचारुशोभा।
कूर्पासकम् परिदधाति नखक्षताङ्गी
व्यालम्बिनीललिलितालककुञ्चिताक्षी।। ४-१६

Another woman, rapturous after making love,
inspects nail marks on her body and her luscious lips,
gleefully puts on her bodice, and lets her soft dark hair
ringlets loose to cover her fluttering eyes. 4-16

अन्यांश्चिरम् सुरतकेलिपरिश्रमेण
खेदम् गताः प्रशिथिलीकृतगात्रयष्टयः।
संहृष्यमाणपुलकोर् उपयोधरान्ता
अभ्यञ्जनम् विदधति प्रमदाः सुशोभाः।। ४-१७

Other charming women weary from prolonged
lovemaking let out soft, joyous sighs,
rubbing oils and pastes on their nipples
and in the deep creases of their thighs. 4-17

बहुगुणरमणीयो योषिताम् चित्तहारी
परिणतबहुशालिव्याकुलग्रामसीमा।
सततम् अतिमनोज्ञः क्रौञ्चमालापरीतः
प्रदिशतु हिमयुक्तः काल एष सुखम् वः।। ४-१८

May this pleasant season of frost,
fields full of golden paddy, sky adorned
with garland of Krauncha birds,
stealing hearts of charming women,
grant you bliss and comfort! 4-18

Krauncha: Demoiselle crane

WINTER

प्ररूढशाल्यंशुचयैर् मनोहरं
क्वचित् स्थितक्रौञ्चनिनादराजितम्।
प्रकामकामम् प्रमदाजनप्रियं
वरोरु कालम् शिशिराह्वयम् शृणु।। ५-१

Winter comes alive in the fields
full of ripened paddy, my love.
Demoiselle cranes let out sweet cries
exhorting lustful women to lose themselves
in the crazy sport of lovemaking. 5-1

निरुद्धवातायनमन्दिरोदरं
हुताशनो भानुमतो गभस्तयः।
गुरूणि वासांस्य् अबलाः सयौवनाः
प्रयान्ति कालेऽत्र जनस्य सेव्यताम्।। ५-२

It's comforting to keep windows shut, fires lit
and bask lazily under the sun, wearing
heavy garments. Men enjoy this season
in the company of grown-up women. 5-2

न चन्दनम् चन्द्रमरीचिशीतला:
नहर्म्यपृष्ठम् शरदिन्दुनिर्मलम्।
न वायव: सान्द्रतुषारशीतला
जनस्य चित्तम् रमयन्ति साम्प्रतम्।। ५-३

Neither sandal paste, cool like moonbeams,
nor breeze chilled by frost,
nor roof tops under the silver moon,
delight people's heart. 5-3

तुषारसङ्घातनिपातशीतलाः
सशाङ्कभाभिः शिशिरीकृताः पुनः।
विपाण्डुतारागणजिह्मभूषिता
जनस्य सेव्या न भवन्ति रात्रयः।। ५-४

Nights embellished with faint star constellations,
are biting cold with frost, and colder still
with the piercing arrows of the moon,
such nights give little joy to the people. 5-4

गृहीतताम्बूलविलेपनस्रजः
मुखासवामोदितवक्त्रपङ्कजाः।
प्रकामकालागुरुधूपवासितं
विशन्ति शय्यागृहम् उत्सुकाः स्त्रियः।। ५-५

Women aching for love, their mouths perfumed
with flower-wine, retire to their bedchambers
filled with fragrance of Kalaguru incense, carrying
betel rolls, chaplets and sensuous perfumes. 5-5

Kalaguru: Black Aloeswood

कृतापराधान् बहुशोऽपि तर्जितान्
सवेपथून् साध्वसलुप्तचेतसः।
निरीक्ष्य भर्तृन् सुरताभिलाषिणः
स्त्रियोऽपराधान् समदा विसस्मरुः।। ५-६

Philandering husbands, who are spurned
and reproached, are forgiven by their wives
thirsting for love, their wrongs forgotten
upon seeing them trembling with guilt and fear. 5-6

प्रकामकामैर् युवभिः सनिर्दयं
निशासु दीर्घास्वभिरामिताश् चिरम्।
भ्रमन्ति मन्दम् श्रमखेदितोरसः
क्षपावसाने नवयौवनाः स्त्रियः॥ ५-७

In the stillness of the long winter nights
the lustful lovers are ruthless in loveplay,
as the night approaches its end, the young women
limp back slowly, drained, their thighs hurting. 5-7

मनोज्ञकूर्पासकपीडितस्तना:
सरागकौशेयकभूषितोरस:।
निवेशितान्त:कुसुमै: शिरोरुहैर्
विभूषयन्तीव हिमागमम् स्त्रिय:।। ५-८

Dazzling like jewels—their voluptuous breasts
held tightly by lovely bodices, their sensuous thighs
covered in colourful silks, fragrant flowers adorning
their hair—women welcome the winter's arrival. 5-8

पयोधरैः कुङ्कुमरागपिञ्जरैः
सुखोपसेव्यैर् नवयौवनोष्मभिः।
विलासिनीभिः परिपीडितोरसः
स्वपन्ति शीतम् परिभूय कामिनः।। ५-९

Young lovers overcome the winter's chill
sleeping together embracing each other tightly,
the chests of lustful men turn ochre from pressing
against the full breasts of amorous women. 5-9

सुगन्धिनिश्वासविकम्पितोत्पलं
मनोहरम् कामरतिप्रबोधकम्।
निशासु हृष्टाः सह कामिभिः स्त्रियः
पिबन्ति मद्यम् सदनीयम् उत्तमम्।। ५-१०

Amorous women sip their choicest wines
along with their lovers during the winter nights,
awakening their passion, their fragrant breath making
the floating lotus petals in the wine glass, quiver. 5-10

अपगतमदरागा योषिद् एका प्रभाते
कृतनिविडकुचाग्रा पत्युर् आलिङ्गनेन।
प्रियतमपरिभुक्तम् वीक्षमाणा स्वदेहं
व्रजति शयनवासाद् वासम् अन्यद् धसन्ती।। ५-११

At the break of the dawn, a young maiden
weary from the night-long love's delight, scans
her squeezed nipples, her body full of love bites,
and moves around with a suppressed smile. 5-11

अगुरुसुरभिधूपामोदितम् केशपाशं
गलितकुसुममालम् तन्वती कुञ्चिताग्रम्।
त्यजति गुरुनितम्बा निम्नमध्यावसाना
उषसि शयनम् अन्या कामिनी चारुशोभाम्।। ५-१२

Another charming woman with deep navel,
curvaceous hips and slender waist,
leaves the bed at the first ray of dawn,
tying her curly hair perfumed with Aguru,
withered flowers from her chaplet falling. 5-12

Aguru: Resin of Aloe Vera

कनककमलकान्तैः साद्य एवाम्बुधौतैः
श्रवणतटनिषक्तैः पाटलोपान्तनेत्रैः।
उषसि वदमबिम्बै रससंसक्तकेशैः
श्रिय इव गृहमध्ये संस्थिता योषितोऽद्य।। ५-१३

Women's oval faces shining like golden lotuses,
their eyelids touching the edge of their ears,
their freshly washed hair dangling over their shoulders,
they resemble goddess Lakshmi seated on her golden lotus,
snuggled in the warm comfort of their homes these days. 5-13

पृथुजघनभरार्ताः किञ्चिद् आनम्रमध्याः
स्तनभरपरिखेदान् मन्दमन्दम् व्रजन्त्यः।
सुरतसमयवेशम् नैशम् आशु प्रहाय
दधति दिवसयोग्यम् वेषम् अन्यास् तरुण्यः।। ५-१४

The young maidens, a little bent down at waists,
bearing the burden of their heavy hips and full bosoms,
walk slowly, but are quick in casting off
their night clothes worn during lovemaking
and changing into garments fit for the day. 5-14

नखपदर्चितभागान् वीक्षमाणाः स्तनाग्रान्
अघरकिसलयाग्रम् दन्तभिन्नम् स्पृशन्त्यः।
अभिमतरसम् एतम् नन्दयन्त्यस् तरुण्यः
सवितुर् उदयकाले भूस्यन्त्याननानि।। ५-१५

At dawn, women scan their bodies
for the love bites, nail marks, touch their
bitten lower lips—tender like fresh leaves,
blushing, they put make-up on their lotus faces. 5-15

प्रचुरगुडविकारः स्वादुशालीक्षुरम्यः
प्रबलसुरतकेलिर् जातकन्दर्पदर्पः।
प्रियजनरहितानाम् चित्तसन्तापहेतुः
शिशिरसमय एष श्रेयसे वोऽस्तु नित्यम्।। ५-१६

Abundant with sweetmeats,
delicious paddy, sugarcane juice,
relentless lovemaking with love-god's blessings,
but heartbreaking for those without lovers,
may this season of winter be auspicious for all! 5-16

SPRING

प्रफुल्लचूताङ्‌कुरतीक्ष्णसायो
द्विरेफमालाविलसद्धनुर्गुणः।
मनांसि वेद्धुम् सुरतप्रसङ्गिनां
वसन्तयोद्धा समुपागतः प्रिये।। ६-१

The warrior spring has come armed,
my love, piercing the hearts of lovers,
new Mango leaves—his sharp arrows,
and row of bees—his shining bowstring. 6-1

द्रुमाः सपुष्पाः सलिलम् सपद्मं
स्त्रियः सकामाः पवनः सुगन्धिः।
सुखाः प्रदोषा दिवसाश् च रम्याः
सर्वम् प्रिये चारुतरम् वसन्ते।। ६-२

Trees are abundant with flowers, ponds with lotuses,
breeze with fragrance, women are full of sensual longing,
days are pleasant, and evenings charming,
everything appears more enticing in spring, my love. 6-2

वापीजलानाम् मणिमेखलानां
शशाङ्कभासाम् प्रमदाजनानाम्।
चूतद्रुमाणाम् कुसुमान्वितानां
ददाति सौभाग्यमयम् वसन्तः।। ६-३

The spring brings good fortune to all
for water in the pools is good for swimming
moonshine feels pleasant, the mango trees have blossomed,
and beautiful women enjoy wearing jeweled girdles. 6-3

कुसुम्भरागारुणितैर् दुकूलैर्
नितम्बबिम्बानि विलासिनीनानाम्।
रक्तांशुकैः कुङ्कुमरागगौरैर्
अलङ्क्रियन्ते स्तनमण्डलानि।। ६-४

Flirtatious women drape silk
dyed in Kusumbha's reddish sap
around their curved hips, and fine silk
tinged with saffron hue adorn their round bosoms. 6-4

Kusumbha: Safflower or Carthamus tinctorius

कर्णेषु योग्यम् नवकर्णिकारं
चलेषु नीलेष्व् अलकेष्व् अशोकम्।
पुष्पम् च फुल्लम् नवमल्लिकायाः
प्रयाति कान्तिम् मदाजनानाम्।। ६-५

Fresh bloom of Karnikaras on their ears,
a chaplet of Ashoka flowers and full blooms
of Navamallika vines on their curly dark hair,
heighten the sensuality of beautiful women. 6-5

Karnikaras: Pterospermum acerifolium or the bayur tree is a flowering plant
Navamallika: Shrubby Jasmine

स्तनेषु हाराः सितचन्दनार्द्रा
भुजेषु सङ्गम् वलयाङ्गदानि।
प्रयान्त्य् अनङ्गातुरमानसानां
नितम्बिनीनाम् जघनेषु काञ्च्यः।। ६-६

Pearl necklaces wet with sandal cream, caress
their full breasts, their favourite armlets
and wristlets kiss their arms, and new girdles
grace the curvaceous hips of women in love. 6-6

सपत्रलेखेषु विलासिनीनाम्
वक्त्रेषु हेमाम्बुरुहोपमेषु।
रत्नान्तरे मौक्तिकसङ्गरम्यः
स्वेदागमो विस्तरताम् उपैति।। ६-७

Faces of sensuous women adorned
with floral designs shine like golden lotuses,
beads of sweat glimmering like pearls,
enhance their beauty even more. 6-7

उच्छ्वासयन्त्यः श्लथबन्धनानि
गात्राणि कंदर्पसमाकुलानि।
समीपवर्तिष्व् अधुना प्रियेषु
समुत्सुका एव भवन्ति नार्यः॥ ६-८

Aroused by the love-god, women
give out soft sighs, the strings
of their lingeries loosened,
they cuddle up with their lovers. 6-8

तनूनि पाण्डूनि समन्थराणि
मुहुर् मुहुर् जृम्भणतत्पराणि।
अङ्गान्य् अनङ्गः प्रमदाजनस्य
करोति लावण्यससम्भ्रमाणि।। ६-९

The immortal love-god makes
pale and thin women, who yawn
again and again, restless with desire,
imparting them beauty and charm. 6-9

नेत्रेषु लोलो मदिरालसेषु
गण्डेषु पाण्डुः कठिनः स्तनेषु।
मध्येषु निम्नो जघनेषु पीनः
स्त्रीणाम् अनङ्गो बहुधा स्थितोऽद्य।। ६-१०

Love-god's charm is evident in women
drunk on wine—their eyes fluttering,
cheeks—glowing, breasts—firm,
waists—slim, and hips—rotund. 6-10

अङ्गानि निद्रालसविभ्रमाणि
वाक्यानि किञ्चिन् मदलालसानि।
भ्रूक्षेपजिह्मानि च वीक्षितानि
चकार कामः प्रमदाजनानाम्।। ६-११

Rendering their bodies full of charm,
love-god makes women drowsy as if drunk on wine,
they speak with a little lisp, their glances slant,
eyelashes drooping and their delicate eyebrows arched. 6-11

प्रियङ्गुकालीयककुङ्कुमाक्तं
स्तनेषु गौरेषु विलासिनीभिः।
आलिप्यन्ते चन्दनम् अङ्गनाभिर्
मदालसाभिर् मृगनाभियुक्तम्।। ६-१२

Beautiful young women, mad with desire,
rub sandal paste on their round bosoms
mixed with saffron, Piryangu, Kaliyaka
and perfume from the navel of the musk deer. 6-12

Priyangu: Aglaia elaeagnoidea or perfumed cherry

Kaliyaka: Coscinium fenestratum or yellow vine is a flowering woody climber

गुरूणि वासांसि विहाय तूर्णं
तनूनि लाक्षारसरञ्जितानि।
सुगन्धिकालागुरुधूपितानि
धत्ते जनः काममदालसाङ्गः।। ६-१३

Ecstatic with the arrival of spring
they take off their heavy winter-wear
and put on their light clothes dyed
in Laksha sap, perfumed with Aguru. 6-13

Laksha: Lac

पुंस्कोकिलश्चूतरसासवेन
मत्तः प्रियाम् चुम्बति रागहृष्टः।
कूजद्विरेफोऽप्य् अयम् अम्बुजस्थः
प्रियम् प्रियायाः प्रकरोति चाटु॥ ६-१४

Crazy cuckoo drunk on Mango nectar,
kisses his mate passionately,
so do the honey bees hidden inside lotus petals,
make love to their sweethearts. 6-14

ताम्रप्रवालस्तवकावनम्राश्
चूतद्रुमाः पुष्पितचारुशाखाः।
कुर्वन्ति कामम् पवनावधूताः
पर्युत्सुकम् मानसम् अङ्गनानाम्।। ६-१५

Mango trees are laden with coppery
tender leaves and slightly bent fresh blooms,
and women ache with desire
watching them swing with the wind. 6-15

आमूलतो विद्रुमरागताम्रं
सपल्लवाः पुष्पचयम् दधानाः।
कुर्वन्त्य् अशोका हृदयम् सशोकं
निरीक्ष्यमाणा नवयौवनानाम्।। ६-१६

Ashoka trees are adorned all over
with fresh coppery flowers and leaves,
the pining hearts of the young
fill with agony watching these. 6-16

मत्तद्विरेफपरिचुम्बितचारुपुष्पा
मन्दानिलाकुलितनम्रमृदुप्रवालाः।
कुर्वन्ति कामिमनसां सहसोत्सुकत्वं
चूताभिरामकलिकाः समवेक्ष्यमाणाः।। ६-१७

The lovelorn hearts of the youngsters are filled
with longing, watching the intoxicated honey bees
kiss the fresh buds of mango trees, whose tendrils
tremble and sway in the gentle spring breeze. 6-17

कान्तामुखद्युतिजुषाम् अपि चोद्गतानां
शोभाम् पराम् कुरवकद्रुममञ्जरीणाम्।
दृष्ट्वा प्रिये सहृदयस्य भवेन् न
कस्य कन्दर्पबाणपतनव्यथितम् हि चेतः।। ६-१८

Which heart can remain untouched by fire
of desire or not be struck by the love-god's arrow,
looking at the unmatched beauty of Kurabaka blossom
rivaling the loveliness of one's beloved's face. 6-18

Kurabaka: A type of Barlaria, Barlaria Prinoitis or the red (or yellow) amaranth

आदीप्तवह्निसदृशैर् मरुतावधूतैः
सर्वत्र किंशुकवनैः कुसुमावनम्रैः।
सद्यो वसन्तसमये हि समाचितेयम्
रक्तांशुका नववधूर् इव भाति भूमिः।। ६-१९

Spring has brought forth groves of flowering
Palasha trees swinging in the wind, bowed
with loads of flowers resembling raging fire
and the earth resembles a newly married bride
dressed in elegant radiant red attire. 6-19

Palasha: Flame of the forest

किम् किंशुकैः शुकमुखच्च्छविभिर् न भिन्नं
किम् कर्णिकारकुसुमैर् न कृतम् नु दग्धम्।
यत् कोकिलः पुनर् अयम् मधुरैर् वचोभिर्
यूनाम् मनः सुवदनानिहितम् निहन्ति।। ६-२०

The sharp red Palasha flowers resembling parrot's beak
have burst forth, there is nothing left to pierce,
anything left is burnt by Karnikara's fiery blossoms,
and now, the joyous cuckoo with its sweet cooing
seals the fate of young hearts lost to amorous women. 6-20

Kimshuka: Palasha or Butea monosperma

Karnikara: Pterospermum acerifolium or the bayur tree is a flowering plant

पुंस्कोकिलैः कलवचोभिर् उपात्तहर्षैः
कूजद्भिर् उन्मदकलानि वचांसि भृङ्गैः।
लज्जान्वितम् सविनयम् हृदयम् क्षणेन
पर्याकुलम् कुलगृहेऽपि कृतम् वधूनाम्।। ६-२१

The hearts of the young, well groomed and polite brides
at their in-laws house, brim with desire, listening
to the rapturous cuckoo singing sweet melodies,
and pleasant humming of the intoxicated bees. 6-21

आकम्पयन् कुसुमिताः सहकारशाखा
विस्तारयन् परभूतस्य वचांसि दिक्षु।
वायुर् विवाति हृदयानि हरन् नराणां
नीहारपातविगमात् सुभगो वसन्ते।। ६-२२

The pleasant spring breeze, free of frost,
blows gently flirting with Mango blossoms,
carrying cuckoo's cooing to a far distance
captivating the hearts of men and women. 6-22

कुन्दैः सविभ्रमवधूहसितावदातैर्
उद्द्योतितान्य् उपवनानि मनोहराणि।
चित्तम् मुनेर् अपि हरन्ति निवृत्तरागं
प्राग् एव रागमलिनानि मनांसि यूनाम्।। ६-२३

The pleasure pavilions alive with Kunda blossoms—
snow white like the sparkling smile of vivacious brides,
enchant the hearts of even dispassionate saints, how can
the lovesick hearts of the young remain unscathed? 6-23

Kunda: A variety of Jasmine

आलम्बिहेमरसनाः स्तनसक्तहाराः
कन्दर्पशिथिलीकृतगात्रयष्ट्यः।
मासे मधौ मधुरकोकिलभृङ्गनादैर्
नार्यो हरन्ति हृदयम् प्रसभम् नराणाम्।। ६-२४

In Chaitra, cuckoo's cooing and humming of bees
fill the air. Women with golden girdles dangling
from their waists, glowing pearl necklaces adorning
their bosoms, their supple bodies ignited by flames of love,
enrapture and ravish the hearts of men, my love. 6-24

Chaitra: The first month of the year in the standard Hindu calendar as well as India's national civil calendar, which usually corresponds to March–April in the Gregorian calendar

नानामनोज्ञकुसुमद्रुमभूषितान्तान्
हृष्टान्य् अपुष्टनिनदाकुलसानुदेशान्।
शैलेयजालपरिणद्धशिलातलौघान्
दृष्ट्वा जनः क्षितिभृतो मुदम् एति सर।। ६-२५

The sight of the hills full of flowering trees,
valleys echoing with cuckoo's cooing,
rocky crevices hosting fragrant mountain moss,
bring joy to the longing eyes, my love. 6-25

नेत्रे निमीलयति रोदिति याति शोकं
करेण विरुणद्धि विरौति चोच्चैः।
कान्तावियोगपरिखेदितचित्तवृत्तिर्
दृष्ट्वाध्वगाः कुसुमितान् सहकारवृक्षान्।। ६-२६

The traveller parted from his lover, seeing
mango trees blooming, finds his eyes welling
up with tears, burning with desire, he covers
his face with his hands and sobs uncontrollably. 6-26

समदमधुभराणां कोकिलानां च नादैः
कुसुमितसहकारैः कर्णिकारैश् च रम्याः।
इषुभिर् इव सुतीक्ष्णैर् मानसं मानिनीनां
तुदति कुसुममासो मन्मथोद्वेजनाय।। ६-२७

The month of flowers—with the humming
of delirious bees, cuckoo's sweet cooing,
blossoming mango and Karnikara flowers
—pierces the hearts of even haughty women,
like love-god's sharp arrows kindling the flame of love. 6-27

Karnikara: Pterospermum acerifolium or the bayur tree is a flowering plant

आम्रीमञ्जुलमञ्जरीवरशरः सत्किंशुकम् यद्धनुर्
ज्या यस्यालिकुलम् कलङ्करहितम् चत्रम् सितांशुः सितम्।
मत्तेभो मलयानिलः परभृतो यद् वन्दिनो लोकजित्
सोऽयम् वो वितरीतरीतु वितनुर् भद्रम् वसन्तान्वितः।। ६-२८

With the veiled arrows of tender Mango blossoms
and the burnishing bow of lovely Palasha blooms,
the row of delirious honey bees—his bowstring,
the pristine parasol of soft moonbeams,
the gentle southerly Malaya breeze—his imperious
elephant, and melodious cuckoos—his singing bards,
may the conqueror of the world, the formless love-god,
along with his bosom buddy Vasanta bring you
and the succeeding generations evermore joy! 6-28

ACKNOWLEDGEMENT

I'm grateful to Chaitali Pandya for reading the manuscript carefully and offering me her valuable suggestions.